creating with **BURLAP**

decorating   painting   embroidering

By M.J. Fressard

STERLING
PUBLISHING CO., INC.   **NEW YORK**
SAUNDERS OF TORONTO, Ltd., Don Mills, Canada

Oak Tree Press Co., Ltd.
Distributed by WARD LOCK, Ltd., London & Sydney

Little Craft Book Series

Translated by Rhea Rollin

Second Printing, 1971
Copyright © 1970 by
Sterling Publishing Co., Inc.
419 Park Avenue South, New York, N.Y. 10016
Simultaneously Published and Copyright © 1970 in Canada
by Saunders of Toronto, Ltd., Don Mills, Ontario
British edition published by Oak Tree Press Co., Ltd.
Distributed in Great Britain and the Commonwealth by
Ward Lock, Ltd., 116 Baker Street, London W1
The original edition was published in France under the title "Avec
de la Toile de Jute" © 1967 by Éditions Sélection J. Jacobs, Paris
Manufactured in the United States of America
All rights reserved
Library of Congress Catalog Card No.: 72-90806
ISBN 0-8069-5144-3   UK 7061 2222 4
5145-1

Contents

4

Before You Begin

Until recently, burlap was used principally in the manufacture of sacks and bags for the storing and transporting of grains and root vegetables, or else it was hidden from sight as a backing material for carpets and rugs. Now, at last, it has emerged and taken its rightful place among other fabrics as a pleasing, versatile cloth for use in original creations as well as a background for painting, embroidery, or tapestries.

Because of its ready availability and modest cost in comparison with other fabrics, burlap has become very popular for school projects as well as for home decoration. Once you have mastered the simple methods and projects in this book, you will certainly be inspired to let your own imagination and taste take over. You will want to make curtains, room dividers, dolls and other toys, artificial flowers, book covers—the ideas are unlimited!

Now, let's get acquainted with some of the characteristics of this exciting, fun-to-work-with fabric.

The Material

Burlap can be obtained in all shops that specialize in materials for arts and crafts and in many that carry household fabrics. It comes in a wide variety of colors, but you can even use old potato sacks provided that they are clean and the threads are not pulled. Burlap is an extremely strong material, although before the threads are woven together, they snap very easily.

Use a mild detergent to wash burlap, and dry it in the shade—dyed burlap tends to fade. Do not allow it to soak for long and add a few drops of vinegar at the final rinsing to revive its sparkle. Burlap does not stretch, but it does shrink a little in washing. However, this can be remedied by ironing it while still slightly damp. [NOTE: Take particular care not to *store* burlap in a damp place, because it has a tendency to rot when over-exposed to moisture.]

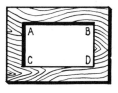

Illus. 1

Experiment: Make a Picture Frame

Choose a picture that you feel will be complemented by the special qualities of burlap. Use a freshly laundered potato sack for your first try. Cut it along the seams so that you have a large, flat piece to work with.

Make a simple frame from four pieces of plywood or cut out from one piece as shown in Illus. 1. The width of the frame should be proportionate to the type of picture you have. The dimensions for the inner edge of the frame should be slightly less than the picture. The pieces can be joined with a staple gun.

5

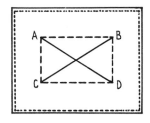

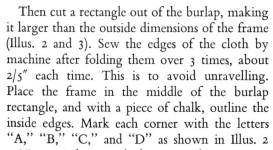

Illus. 2

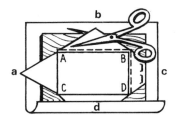

Illus. 3. Rear view.

Then cut a rectangle out of the burlap, making it larger than the outside dimensions of the frame (Illus. 2 and 3). Sew the edges of the cloth by machine after folding them over 3 times, about 2/5″ each time. This is to avoid unravelling. Place the frame in the middle of the burlap rectangle, and with a piece of chalk, outline the inside edges. Mark each corner with the letters "A," "B," "C," and "D" as shown in Illus. 2

Now stitch around the rectangle A-B-C-D along the chalked lines. (This will prevent unravelling when you cut out the rectangle.) Then make chalk lines on the diagonals of the rectangle as shown in Illus. 2. Cut along the diagonals.

Place the frame on the burlap (Illus. 3). (Keep in mind that you are working on the *back* side of the frame.) If the diagonals are short of the four corners, snip them until they are even with the wood. Pull the four pointed flaps back (*a*). If the pointed ends extend beyond the frame, cut them as shown in Illus. 3 (*b*) so they are flush with the wood edges. Then staple as shown at *c*.

Now turn the excess burlap in and over the flaps (*d*) until snug, and staple them to the back of the frame. Place your picture in the frame carefully and provide it with a strong backing of cardboard which you will also staple down. Attach a picture hook or a nail and your picture frame is complete.

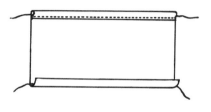

Illus. 4. Instead of buying new furniture, re-decorate your home by covering the lamp shades with bright burlap.

A Lamp Shade

Now that you have the "feel" of the burlap—how it reacts to handling and cutting, you can try a more ambitious project—a burlap lamp shade. You may want to use a more decorative color than the natural tone—but remember that the light must come through so do not choose too dark a color. Our lamp shade in Illus. 4 has an Italian wine-bottle base, and the straw harmonizes well with the texture of the burlap.

For the framework of the shade, you can use either a ready-made white paper shade or make one yourself from a large piece of manila tag. This heavy card stock is thin and supple enough to form into a cylinder and stiff enough to hold its shape. Join the two ends with transparent adhesive tape.

Now cut out a rectangle from your burlap. The length should be equal to the perimeter of the shade, *plus* $1\frac{1}{2}''$. The width should be equal to the height of the shade, *plus* 3".

On each long side fold the burlap over $1\frac{1}{2}''$ (Illus. 5) and pin down with straight pins. Insert very fine wire through each "hem," and then stitch tightly by machine. Then sew the two ends together so that they form a kind of muff shown in Illus. 6. Slip this over the shade, pull the wires top and bottom so that the burlap is shirred and fits over the shade as shown in Illus. 4. Twist the wires together and snip off any loose ends.

7

A Carryall

Illus. 6

After completing your lamp shade you might try making a plain burlap carryall for a child. Cover a cylinder of cardboard in the same way as you did the shade. However, allow additional material top and bottom. Insert heavy wire at the bottom and pull the burlap together tightly. A big colorful pompon can be sewn on to hide the shirred joining as shown in Illus. 7. Use a heavy white cord at the top as a drawstring.

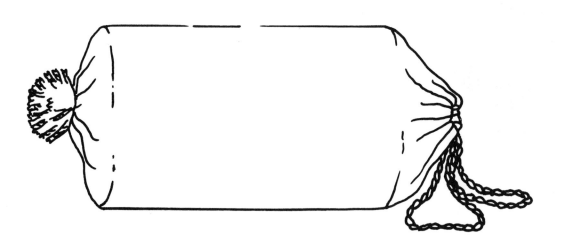

Illus. 7. A doll's suitcase, a picnic basket or a pocketbook—a child's imagination sees many uses for this easy burlap carryall!

Illus. 8. Even a child can create with burlap. Painting the fabric is an art that anyone can do.

Painting on Burlap

Two charming examples of painted burlap done by children are shown in Illus. 8 and Illus. 9. These paintings make cheerful small wall hangings in children's bedrooms, playrooms or schoolrooms. (See the back cover for the color effect in Illus. 9.)

Before you start such a project it is wise to experiment with the design on paper. Then cut out the paper patterns and trace them with chalk on to the burlap. In this way, you will not make mistakes that would be very difficult—if not impossible—to correct on the cloth.

You can consult your arts and crafts supplier about the most suitable paint for the burlap you purchase. Acrylic polymer paints are very satisfactory. These should be applied over a base of acrylic emulsion gesso which provides a smooth white surface upon which to paint and upon which you can sketch your designs. It acts as both a sizing and a primer and is not absorbed into the porous burlap. In addition, it dries very quickly and you can start to paint within an hour!

Be sure to work the gesso well into the weave. Use a fairly wide brush—$\frac{1}{2}''$ to $1''$—since your painting should tend to be broad rather than detailed. Fussy little areas are not well suited to the rustic character of the burlap.

An absolute must when working with these paints is to have the burlap immaculately clean before you begin. Soil of any kind, particularly grease, will undermine the effectiveness of the emulsion base and cause deterioration.

Illus. 9. The child who painted this divided the area into small sections to tell a story.

The care of your painted burlap is limited to two important points:

1. Washing: NEVER immerse in water. DO use a moist sponge dipped in fluffy mild suds to gently wash the painted areas. RINSE quickly with another clean, *moist* sponge several times.

2. Handling: NEVER roll up a painted burlap piece with the painted side *in*. ALWAYS roll up with the painted side *out*. The paint will crack if compressed.

For a large decorative panel such as the tale of Little Red Riding Hood in Illus. 9, you may wish to make a frame. Instructions for frames are given on page 38. If you simply tack the hanging, be sure to stitch a hem all round the burlap to prevent unravelling.

Draping and Shaping

Draping is one of the most exciting things you can do with burlap. All you will need is white glue, water, and aluminium foil, and you can make all kinds of figures—dolls, animals, flowers, etc.

Try making a simple doll as shown in Illus. 11, using a pre-shaped plastic foam cone for the body and a ball for the head. If you want, you can use stiff wire, such as a coat hanger, instead.

Lay out a large sheet of aluminium foil. Thin the glue by adding water at the ratio of 5 parts glue to 1 part water.

Let's make a doll 12″ tall with a 10″ cone and a 2″ head. Cut out an 11″ square from red burlap. Cut it to the shape shown in Illus. 10A. Place it on the sheets of aluminium foil and brush the glue mix on to it. Turn over and brush the other side. Make sure it is thoroughly coated. Drape it round the cone so that it overlaps in the back. Stitch it together at the neck. Adjust the dress in any way that you please.

Then cut out two more pieces which you will stitch on as sleeves. Make them 8″ × 6″ and cut in the shape of a triangle (Illus. 10B). Soak them in the glue mix as before and roll them into two cones and shape them. Then sew on at the neck.

You can paint the facial features on the head and attach yarn for hair. Let your doll dry for several days on the aluminium foil and you will find her dress has assumed a stiff, but flexible, quality.

An important thing to remember is never to squeeze the wet burlap. If you have an excess of glue, simply press it out. If you squeeze it, you will form permanent wrinkles.

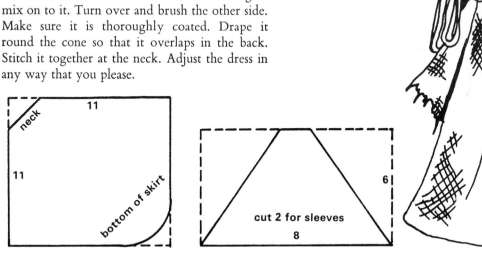

Illus. 11

11
neck

11

bottom of skirt

Illus. 10 A

cut 2 for sleeves

6

8

Illus. 10 B

11

Burlap Backgrounds

As a background material, burlap is unsurpassed—it provides texture, color, and a surface upon which you can either sew or glue other fabrics or materials of any kind. You can use all sorts of cloth remnants—plain or patterned, cotton or wool. All you need is a design, a pair of scissors and glue.

Cloth Pictures

Make the harlequin in Illus. 12 in the following way. First, draw his outline on a large sheet of heavy paper and cut it out in one piece. Then lay the figure on a large piece of plain or pastel burlap and trace in chalk.

Now, take the figure and trace it on to a large piece of material such as cotton of one color only, say, yellow. Cut this out and lay it on the burlap outline. When you are sure you are satisfied with the figure and its placement, glue the cloth to the burlap with a glue recommended for textiles.

Then, in the same way, make paper patterns of the smaller details, such as the hat, the flowers and the bird, and transfer them to varicolored cloth pieces and glue in place. After all of the general outlines are in place, use your paper patterns to plan the designs of the suit, the hat, plume, flower parts, etc. Then cut out each piece accordingly and glue on to the fabric.

Illus. 13 and Illus. 14 are both examples of the use of burlap as a background for decorative

Illus. 12. This colorful harlequin was made from scraps of cloth sewn onto a burlap backing.

scenes. This busy village scene is composed of felt pieces glued on to a long strip of burlap. Notice that much of the charm of the scene is achieved through the imaginative use of shapes and sizes—for example, birds are almost as large as cars, trees tower over houses.

Felt is an excellent companion for burlap because of its texture and the many colors available. It is also a very easy material to work with. For a scene such as this, the various parts—houses, animals, cars, flowers—can all be cut out

Illus. 13. The felt pieces here are not cut with exact detail.

and then moved around on the burlap until the most satisfying arrangement is achieved before glueing down. It is not necessary to lay out a carefully planned design.

The jolly scene in Illus. 15 is composed of many different kinds of fabric and designs glued on burlap. Remember though, as in making a patchwork quilt, even though you might use a great variety of colors and shapes, you must maintain harmony or the result will be garish. As in Illus. 13 and 14, the disproportionate sizes of the various elements create a charming effect.

Illus. 14. The imperfections add to the charm of the design and make it cheerful and carefree.

Illus. 15. Bits of various fabrics should be tastefully arranged to avoid clashing. But don't be afraid to experiment!

String Pictures

String combines well with burlap because of its texture, and it is easy for children to work with. They can create all kinds of pictures on a burlap background—realistic, fanciful, or abstract designs.

The elegant bird in Illus. 16 was outlined on the burlap in chalk. Then the string was laid down on the outline—a number of different pieces were required as you can see in the photograph. The string was stitched on to the burlap with large simple overcast (couching) stitches of a matching thread. You might want to use different colored yarns to make your bird, as well as colored burlap.

However, do not stop with making a bird—go on to making all kinds of string pictures. You might even want to stitch together two or four different-colored pieces of burlap to use as a background, particularly if you use only one color string or yarn and your design is simple.

Illus. 16. Draw a whimsical design on the burlap, and cover the lines with simple stitches. The result may pleasantly surprise you!

Montages

You can make a nature picture on a green burlap background. Collect dried grasses, pine cones, twigs, dead leaves, and dried flowers and pin or glue to the burlap. Be sure that all of your plant life is thoroughly dried out.

Or, if you are interested in insect life, you can create a fascinating montage of your collection of specimens—butterflies, beetles, etc. Instead of merely lining them up, make a nature scene by placing them in such a way that they appear as they might in life—butterflies in the air, beetles and caterpillars crawling on the ground.

If you are really ambitious, you can combine them with the dried plant life. If you do, why not stitch two pieces of burlap together—one light blue, the other green—representing the sky and the grass? Then you can add a large yellow felt sun or a small blue pond. The possibilities are unlimited—once you begin, more and more ideas will come to you.

Illus. 17. Instead of copying nature with fabric, use real leaves and twigs to create your own miniature forest.

16

Decorating Burlap
by Reweaving

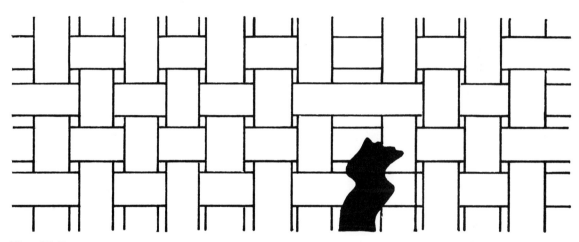

Illus. 18. Because the burlap is loosely woven, one individual thread can easily be removed and replaced with a different color.

Reweaving with
Colored Thread or Wool

In reweaving you simply replace certain burlap threads with other threads or materials. The stitches and methods are easy enough for children to do. First, you very carefully pull out a burlap thread. You will notice that there is a kind of "ladder" left consisting of large and small "rungs" (Illus. 18). The replacing thread should be passed

17

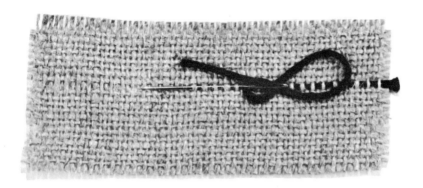

Making a Design

over the large rungs and under the small ones as shown in Illus. 19 and 20. Then remove the next thread and replace it in the same way. A twisted cotton or wool thread of medium thickness is ideal for this work.

Once you have mastered the simple replacement of threads you can make different designs by varying the threading process. Instead of over 1 and under 1, try passing 1 thread over, 3 threads under:

Illus. 20. Diagram of replacing a thread.

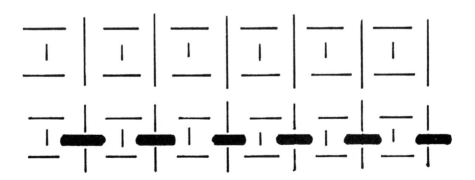

or 3 threads over, 1 thread under:

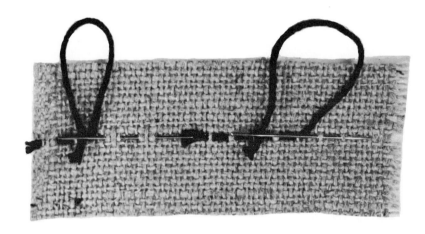

Illus. 21. Pass the new color under 3 or over 3 burlap threads to create a pattern.

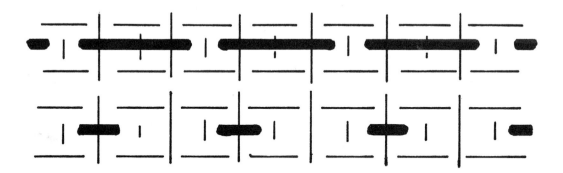

In the same way, you could pass 3 threads over, 3 threads below; 5 threads over, 1 thread below, or any number of combinations. However, two cardinal rules must be observed: *Pull out only one thread at a time* and *always count odd numbers of threads*—1, 3, 5, etc. If you do not go over or under an odd number of threads, the remaining burlap threads will be too loose (see Illus. 22).

19

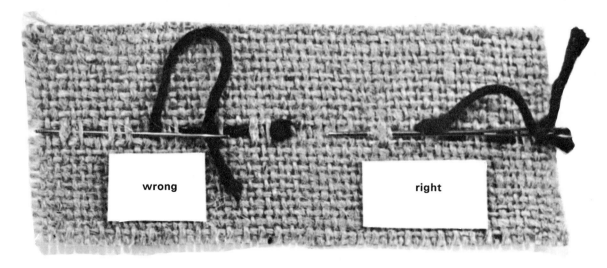

Illus. 22. This time, the color is going over 3 threads, and then under 3. Remember to skip only an odd number of threads, never an even number.

Reweaving with Lace or Embroidered Trimming

This material can be purchased at variety stores, is very inexpensive and comes in all different patterns, sizes, and colors. The principle is the same as replacing threads. Although you will have to pull several threads to allow for the width of the replacing material, remember still to pull only one at a time and do so very carefully.

Also, abide by the rule of odd-number threading as before. In this case, it will have to be fairly large numbers, such as 5 and 7, in order to allow

the trim to show off to its best advantage. Lace or trim that is fairly stiff is most satisfactory. It should not be too wide.

You must sew the ends to the burlap. Since you will probably be making a hem if you make a napkin such as in Illus. 25, turn the ends under and use the herringbone stitch to finish it (Illus. 30). You will find this stitch very handy in finishing such articles as small panels, napkins that are not fringed, or place mats.

Illus. 23. Vary the color of the thread and length of the stitches to achieve a pleasing design. This piece could be a bureau scarf or placemat.

Illus. 24. To make a fringe, brush glue onto the wrong side of the article in a $\frac{1}{4}$-inch strip. Pull threads loose up to the glued area. If the article is washed, take care to reglue, as threads will pull easily.

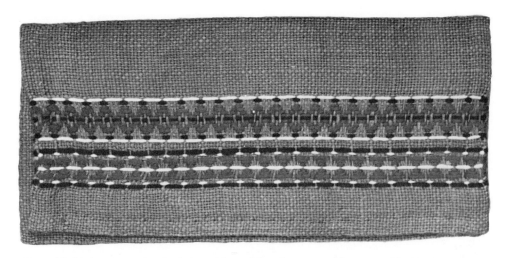

Illus. 25. Make a set of colorful napkins, either for yourself or as a gift. Hem the edges securely with the herringbone stitch, as these will get a lot of use.

Illus. 26. With its bright yarns and zigzag pattern, this piece looks almost like an Indian design.

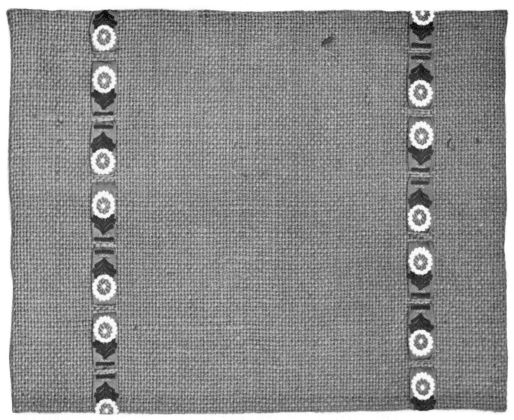

Illus. 27. In addition to yarn, laces and trims can also be rewoven into burlap by removing several threads. Be careful when removing the original strands, as the fabric will be quite fragile.

A Decorated Duffel

A duffel bag such as the one in Illus. 29 can be used for all sorts of purposes—as a beachbag, a utility bag, or even as a book bag for a child. Since it will have a sturdy base and be of double thickness, it will be capable of withstanding heavy weights and constant use.

Cut a circle 6″ in diameter from a piece of plywood or very heavy cardboard, depending upon how sturdy you want your bag to be. This will form the base of the bag (Illus. 28 A). Then cut two burlap circles, one 7″ in diameter and one 9″ in diameter. Stitch the edges of these circles to prevent unravelling.

24

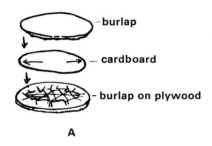

burlap

cardboard

burlap on plywood

A

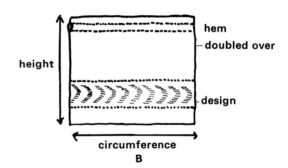

height

circumference

hem

doubled over

design

B

Place the wood or cardboard circle on the large (9″) circle. Fold the burlap edge over the wood and stitch the burlap together so that it holds the piece of wood. You could also staple it down. Cut out another, somewhat smaller and lighter weight, piece of cardboard and glue this on. Then take the second (7″) piece of burlap and sew it on to the edges of the first piece. The base of the bag is complete.

Next, cut out two burlap rectangles, each 16″ × 19″ (Illus. 28 B). Take one of them and reweave in whatever design you choose. Our bag has nine different pieces of trim which form a symmetrical pattern starting from the middle. The extent of the decorated area is up to you. Once the reweaving is complete, line the burlap with the second piece by stitching them together tightly. The circumference (19″) of the burlap when the ends are held together should be equal to the circumference of the 6″ base which you made.

To make the "slot" for the drawstring, measure from the top $1\frac{1}{2}$″ and stitch the two pieces together in two rows 1″ or more apart (Illus. 28 B), and pull the previously sewn threads at each end to make eyelets. Sew round the eyelets with a

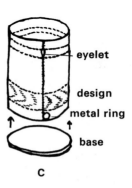

eyelet

design

metal ring

base

C

Illus. 28. Construction of a duffel.

buttonhole stitch to prevent unravelling (Illus. 28 C). Use a heavy white cord for the drawstring. The bag in Illus. 29 has a metal ring sewn on to the base through which the cord was put before it was inserted into the burlap. This way it becomes a shoulder bag.

To complete the bag, simply sew the two 16″ sides together and then stitch the resulting cylinder to the base.

Embroidering Burlap

Whether you do simple embroidering or more complicated stitches, you will always be delighted with the results. You can decorate all kinds of burlap objects, even the lamp shade on page 7.

Only a few basic stitches are necessary to make the projects here. We have chosen those which are best suited for work with burlap and to the manual ability of children. Practice your stitching on pieces of scrap burlap until you can do them easily before tackling a finished piece. Use a large needle with a large, long eye and a fairly blunt point.

If you wish to, although it is not necessary, you can use a canvas stretcher when embroidering on the burlap. These can be acquired in art supply houses. The burlap is stretched over the stretcher bars and held in place with tacks. However, if you intend to mount your piece, the stretcher will serve this purpose and you will only need to provide a frame (see page 38).

Illus. 29. Carry your things to the beach or a picnic in this duffel. If you wish, line it with plastic to make it leakproof.

Illus. 30. The herringbone stitch is the basic hem stitch.

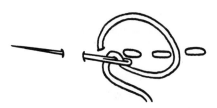

Illus. 31. The herringbone stitch. Move the needle in the direction opposite your over-all sewing: if you are going right, take right-to-left stitches.

Designs

There are several ways of transferring your chosen designs on to the burlap before beginning embroidering, or later on, doing tapestry on burlap. You have already used the chalk method in painting. However, for more detail, you might

Illus. 32. The running stitch is the easiest stitch. To keep your work neat, both stitch and space should be the same length.

Illus. 33. In the cross stitch, work all diagonals in one direction, then reverse and complete the crosses.

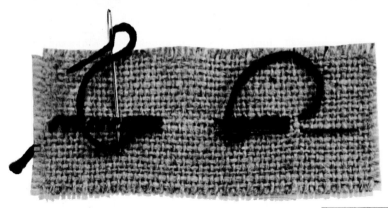

Illus. 34. The cross stitch.

want to make your design on tissue paper. Then pin the paper on the burlap and baste the tissue to the burlap along all the outlines of the design with running stitches (Illus. 32). After sewing, you will be able to tear the tissue away. When your embroidering is complete, remove the basting stitches. Use white thread so it will be easily distinguished.

Still another way is to use dressmaker's carbon paper, which is non-smearing. Lay the carbon on the burlap and place your paper design on it. Trace all the lines of the design with a ballpoint pen or other blunted implement. Do not press too hard or you will tear the carbon. This method is best suited for lighter colors since the transferred lines will not show up on very dark burlap.

If the design you have chosen is small and you wish to enlarge it, or vice versa, use the "squaring off" method shown in Illus. 35.

Illus. 35. To enlarge a pattern, "square it off."
Draw your design on paper and divide the area into squares. On another sheet of paper, draw larger squares, and copy the design of each square into the corresponding larger square.

28

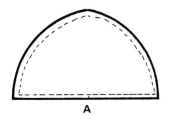 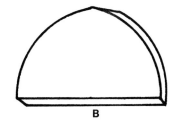 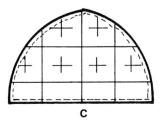

A   **B**   **C**

Illus. 36. Pattern for a teapot cover.

The Cross Stitch

This stitch is also referred to as the "sampler" stitch, and is very easy to do as well as being attractive. Work slanting stitches from right to left, or top to bottom, and then reverse and make the crosses, going back to the starting point. Make sure you go over the same number of threads for each stitch and that your cross stitches always go in the same direction; otherwise, the effect will be spoiled. See Illus. 33 and 34.

Make a Teapot Cover

The handsome teapot cover in Illus. 37 has been embroidered with a design composed of the cross stitch. It is made up of three separate sections, each of which are three layers thick.

Take the measurements of your teapot or kettle and make a paper pattern in the shape shown in Illus. 36.

Cut out this pattern as follows:
A. 3 times from burlap
B. 3 times from nylon netting or felt
C. 3 times from burlap.

Illus. 37. An ornamental cover for the teapot will add charm to your kitchen! Make a floppy tassel for the top.

Illus. 38. The cross stitch is very even because it carefully follows the weaving of the fabric.

Embroider with your cross-stitch design on the 3 pattern C pieces. This will form the outside of the cover. Stitch the edges of all 3 pattern A pieces and all 3 pattern C pieces to prevent unravelling.

Then take one of the pattern A pieces and stitch one of the nylon or felt interlinings to it. (If you wish, make 6 pieces of pattern B and use a double thickness for the lining. This will give you a plumper, softer cover.)

When all three pieces are ready, stitch them together, preferably by machine, on the wrong side—that is, the inside. They will form a little inside-out tent. The bottom will be open. Then turn them right-side out and you have an em-

Illus. 39. Before you stitch, plan your pattern on graph paper. This will insure straight rows and a symmetrical pattern.

Illus. 40 (left) and 41 (below). Cotton thread instead of yarn creates a more detailed pattern. Stitch animals and people using different colors to shade or highlight certain areas.

broidered burlap teapot cover, fancy enough for any tea party. You can add a yarn pompon on top as a decorative handle.

The Holbein Stitch

The Holbein stitch (Illus. 42 and 45), which is also called the double-running stitch, is worked all around the design in one direction. Then another row is worked back over the same area, filling in the spaces and resulting in the same effect on both the back and front of the fabric.

As you can see in Illus. 42, the design has been worked from right to left, with the embroidering thread passing over 3 burlap threads. This stitch

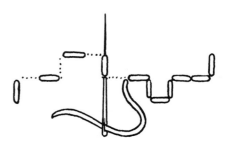

Illus. 42. The Holbein stitch is a row of running stitches with the spaces filled in by another row of running stitches. The stitch can also be done in a straight line.

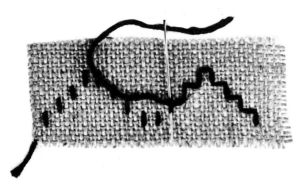

combines well with the cross stitch, as shown in the bottom design in Illus. 44.

A Holbein-Stitched Handbag

Decide upon the size you wish your handbag to be. Then from colored burlap (pale pink with black and white embroidery would make a lovely summer bag), cut a rectangle more than *twice* the size. For instance, if you decide upon a 14″ × 7″ bag, cut a piece 30″ × 15″. Fold it in two along the 30″ width (Illus. 43) and set the fold by ironing it with a steam iron. Then about 2″ from either side of the fold begin your embroidery with the Holbein stitch as shown in Illus. 44.

You might wish to border the stitching on each side with a band of rewoven trim or with the chain stitch (Illus. 46, page 33). When you have finished your embroidery, line the burlap with

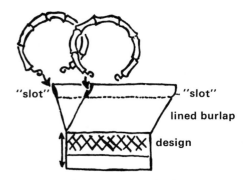

Illus. 43. Construction of a handbag.

either another piece of burlap or with a piece of scrap cloth. Stitch together well—material linings often have a tendency to pull away.

Along each of the 30″ sides stitch a 1″ hem using the herringbone stitch (page 27). This hem will hold the handles (Illus. 43). Then fold the burlap over, turn inside out and stitch the two 15″ sides as far as the top of the embroidery as shown in Illus. 43. You can obtain bamboo handles, such as we have used, in hobby shops, or you might want to have a simple drawstring. When you insert the handles in the ends, they will draw the burlap together as shown in Illus. 44.

Illus. 44. Use many different stitches to make a colorful handbag which will be frequently admired.

32

Illus. 45. "Steps" of the Holbein stitch are inside one another to make an optical pattern that dazzles the eye.

The Chain Stitch

This stitch is one of the most useful in making lines and outlines as well as a solid filling. You must practice this stitch to make the chain links as perfect as possible.

Bring the needle through to the right side of the fabric and make a loop with the thread (Illus. 46), holding it down with your finger. Begin the next stitch from the hole through which the needle last emerged, making a small stitch within

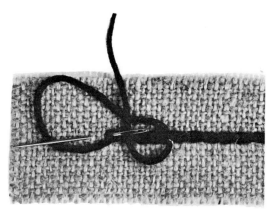

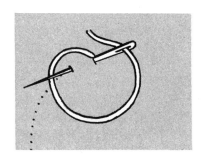

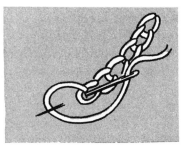

Illus. 46. Each chain stitch should be round and even. Since the stitch can be used for either an outline or a solid filling, it is worth extra effort to perfect it.

33

Illus. 47. A symmetrical design like this one should be carefully planned before you thread the needle. It is easier to change the pattern on paper than it is to undo your stitches.

the loop and drawing the needle out over the thread.

You should have a row of back stitches on the reverse side while on the design side the stitches should be even and loose to prevent the burlap from puckering.

A Chain-Stitched Pillow

The stuffed burlap pillow in Illus. 47 is decorated with black, green and rust yarn in a design composed of the chain stitch.

You can make this pillow in any size you wish.

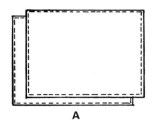

A

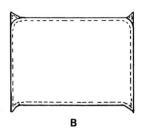

B

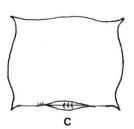

C

Illus. 48. Steps in making a pillow.

Cut out two pieces of burlap in this size, *plus* 1″
all round. Stitch the edges of both pieces (Illus.
48 A) to prevent unravelling.

Transfer your pattern to one burlap piece, or
both if you wish, using one of the methods
described on page 27. Then work the embroidery
in the chain stitch.

Place the two parts with their *right* sides against
each other and stitch them together by machine,
leaving an opening for stuffing (Illus. 48 B). The
pillow cover will then be inside out. Turn it right-
side out and insert a pencil through the opening
and poke it into the four corners to make them
stand up (Illus. 48 C) as they will be inverted.

Stuff with whatever material you like, making
sure you use enough so the pillow will be packed.
Then, stitch the opening closed.

A Toy Turtle

The busy swimmer in Illus. 49 is made of red
and white burlap and is embroidered with heavy
wool in the chain stitch. Make your turtle as large
as possible. Cut each of the patterns in Illus. 49 A
out twice—once from red burlap and once from
white burlap. The red will form the top and the
white will be the bottom.

Embroider the shell, using black and white wool
yarn, either in the design shown here or in one
of your own choosing. However, keep it simple—
this toy is meant to be played with and sat on.

Place the two corresponding pieces of each of
the parts together so that when you stitch them
they will be inside out. Stitch by machine if
possible since the turtle may receive rough hand-

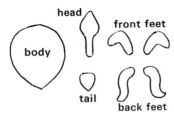

head
front feet
body
tail
back feet

Illus. 49A

**assembled turtle
seen from beneath**

Illus. 49B

ling. Leave ample openings through which you can stuff. Then turn each piece right-side out and stuff with soft material—cotton batting would be ideal. Stitch up the openings and then sew the various parts to each other.

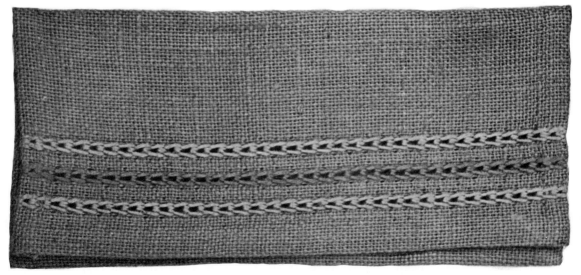

Illus. 50. A napkin decorated with the double chain stitch.

The Double-Chain Stitch

The embroidery on the napkin in Illus. 50 is made with the double chain. This stitch is especially attractive for such things as place mats, curtains, napkins, and so forth.

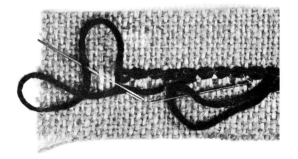

Illus. 51. The double-chain stitch is an interesting variation of the chain stitch.

Illus. 52. Embroider several stitches for varied effects. The handle on this pin cushion can be held even when full of pins.

Begin as for the chain stitch: Form a loop towards the left, restitch at the starting point, go *under* 3 threads. Then return to the inside of the loop, hold the thread, form the loop towards the left, stitch *under* the first loop (not inside). Again go 3 threads under beyond the second loop and continue as before.

When you are ready to go back the other way, simply place the loop towards the right instead of the left.

Combined Stitchery

All the stitches here can be combined. The little pin cushion which is shown in Illus. 52 is embroidered with different stitching. Try to envision the final effect when combining stitches and avoid too elaborate a design. Cluttered, heavy-looking embroidery is very unattractive and the nature of burlap demands simplicity.

Always test out your combinations before working on a finished project and you will always be pleased with the results.

Tapestry on Burlap

True tapestry is a special and ancient technique devoted mainly to large wall hangings, where the front and back surfaces are the same and the background material is completely covered. However, as you will see, you can apply certain basic stitches to burlap and achieve the same surface effect. You may wish to work with the burlap on a stretcher (see page 26), but it is not absolutely necessary.

Carefully plan your design before you begin—the colors as well as the lines. Do this on paper by first cutting out a paper pattern of the general outlines and then cutting out all of the individual elements of the design, one by one, and transferring them to the burlap using one of the methods described on page 27. You can label each part with the color you intend to use. Or better, color each part with crayon so you can be sure your finished work will be exactly as you want it to be.

Frames

For large wall hangings over 30″, such as the tapestries on these pages, you might wish to

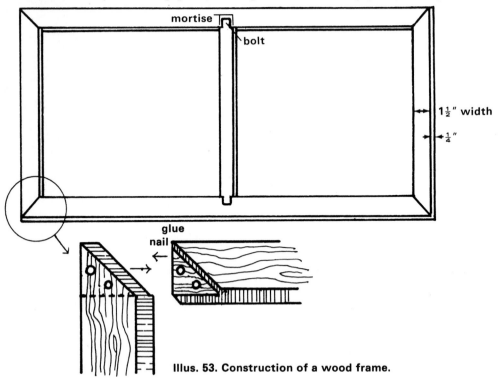

Illus. 53. Construction of a wood frame.

mortise

bolt

1½″ width

¼″

glue

nail

make a frame. To make the frame shown in Illus. 53, allow 1″ all round the burlap when you plan your design. Stitch the edges to keep them from unravelling.

Make the frame as shown in Illus. 53, according to the dimensions of your piece and nail the finished work on the back.

The Satin Stitch

This is the best and easiest stitch to use for your burlap tapestry. It covers the material and provides a smooth, continuous surface. As you can see in Illus. 54, the yarn follows a "lane" formed by two burlap threads, passing under the material, and emerges at another line. Then it is carried back to the starting point. The important thing to remember is to keep these long stitches even and each equally taut. If you do not, the thread will be scraggly and the design will be spoiled.

The stitch can be worked either horizontally or vertically (Illus. 57). Decide which direction

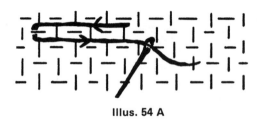

Illus. 54 A

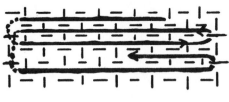

Illus. 54 B

you wish the thread to go. Do not make stitches longer than 1″. If the part of the design you are working is relatively small, you can make it with

Illus. 55. The satin stitch has a very smooth surface.

Illus. 56. If the area is large, make 2 or 3 stitches in a row.

39

single stitches (Illus. 55). However, if it is larger, you must break the area up with individual 1″ stitches. The light area in Illus. 56 is composed of single stitches. Beginning with the dark area, the

Illus. 57. Lots of bright colors would attract any child to this perky duck.

design is broken up into two joining stitches. On an even larger area, make as many stitches as necessary.

We show many examples on these pages of tapestry on burlap using the satin stitch—Most of these charming articles were created by young children!

A Tapestry Duck

To make the fantasy duck in Illus. 57, draw a paper pattern of one side of the body. (You will make the legs and beak later.) Then transfer this pattern to a double thickness of brightly colored burlap, perhaps orange, and cut. You will have two pieces exactly the same.

Using the satin stitch, decorate the two halves either following our pattern or with one of your own. Do use a colorful assortment of threads.

Then stitch the two halves together, right-side in, leaving an opening along the chest section for stuffing. Turn right-side out and stuff with cotton batting.

Make the feet and a beak from stiff wire, poke them well into the burlap stuffing, and cover them by winding red yarn or heavy thread round them.

Our duck is 10″ high and has a blue collar trimmed with rust-colored stitches and a blue crest. But you can make him any size or color you want. You might wish to make a very large one as a decorative touch for a children's room. Try making other stuffed animals in the same way.

Illus. 58. The satin stitch completely covers the threads of the burlap. This piece is symmetrical in shape, but the colors are opposite.

Illus. 59. An imaginary flower grows from a heart-shaped flower pot.

Illus. 60. (right) This picture is striking because of its lack of symmetry and bright colors. Both horizontal and vertical satin stitches were used.

43

Illus. 61 and 62. Add a cheerful note to your kitchen by making pot holders with unusual designs! Put a backing on the burlap so the holder is thick enough.

Illus. 63. By outlining the colored areas with a dark color, you can make a tapestry that resembles stained glass.

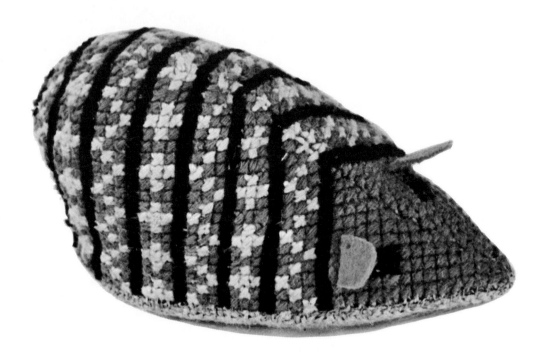

Illus. 64. Just for fun, make a pin cushion with a bit of life to it. This porcupine looks as if he might run away!

The Cross Stitch

For small tapestry articles, the cross stitch, which is described on page 27, is particularly suited. Since the stitches are small compared to the satin stitch, it would be far too time-consuming to use it to cover an entire large object. However, the porcupine pin cushion in Illus. 64 is easy to cover, and the cross stitch allows for a colorful design in such a limited area.

A Porcupine Pin Cushion

Looking at Illus. 64, you probably see a mouse. However, when this little creature fulfils its purpose—that of holding pins and needles, he is transformed into a porcupine!

You will need to make three parts as shown in the patterns in Illus. 65. Make the two sides 3″ from front to back and the base 2½″, because the sides will have to curve round in the back to meet each other.

First stitch the two sides together along their top lines. Then stitch each side to the base. Leave an opening at the rear for stuffing. Then work the cross-stitch design over the entire body, which you will have marked with the outlines of the design as well as the colors. Add two little felt ears and your porcupine is ready to go to work.

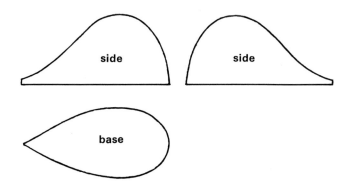

Illus. 65. Pattern for a porcupine pin cushion.

Index